*To kids of all ages who find it exciting
to get up and do things for themselves ...those
who respect their creative talents
and are willing to push them to the limits.*

Special thanks to my mom Dolores,
for never barring me from the kitchen when I was a kid.

Susan and David for their never-ending encouragement.

Kimberly Simon, my bread-baking sidekick since
she was seven, and whose suggestions and instructions
I dutifully followed.

Shane Hardiman, who at age ten, gave up
many hours with the guys to test and retest the
recipes contained here-in.

Avery,
I used this in my classsroom. I hope you enjoy it
Love
Grandma
2019

UNCLE GENE'S
BREADBOOK FOR KIDS!

Step-by-step instruction in the art of bread-baking
—without the use of electrical mixers.

HAPPIBOOK PRESS
MONTGOMERY, NEW YORK

First printing June 1986
Second printing August 1988

Published by Happibook Press,
P.O. Box 218, Montgomery, New York 12549-0218
Manufactured in the United States of America.

ISBN 0-937395-00-5

Table of contents

Who in the world is Uncle Gene?

RON VILLEGAS

Who, you may ask, is "Uncle Gene" Bové and how on earth did he create this perfectly wonderful breadbook for kids?

Gene is a former art director who spent 25 years in advertising, the last 20 at BBDO, making warm and witty print and television ads for clients like Campbell Soup, Pillsbury and Quaker Oats.

Two years ago he chose to leave Madison Avenue at the peak of his career to write and illustrate children's books on his farm in upstate New York.

Gene's choice of a second career was a natural for a man who loves cooking and baking and writing and drawing—and kids.

The creation of this, his first published book, has been a labor of love to which Gene has devoted his spare time and energy for many years—developing, revising, testing and sampling his recipes with the joyful assistance of the dozens of kids who've been lucky enough to share in the fun of baking with Uncle Gene.

Now we can all share in the fun—kids and grown-ups alike—while we wait with impatience for Gene's next book, and the next, and the next.

Mary Ellen Campbell
Sr. Vice President,
Creative Director, BBDO Inc.

A note to parents

What tastes more delicious or has a more mouth-watering aroma than fresh baked bread?

And would it not taste that much better if it was baked by your child!

Sometimes thought to be a difficult task, bread-baking need not be. With your encouragement and guidance your child will find the experience a joy. It will open his mind creatively while giving him a sure sense of accomplishment and pride as he shares the fruits of his labor with family and friends.

The recipes are kept as simple as possible, with easy to follow step-by-step instruction. No electrical mixers are used. The hand utensils are found in most homes. At times your child may need a little help with the hand blending or kneading of the dough, but I have found that after age ten or eleven a child can accomplish this task easily on his own.

The recipes are for conventional, not microwave ovens.

I'm confident that you will enjoy your child's bread baking experience as much as your child.

– E.B.

P.S. This special printing of Uncle Gene's Breadbook For Kids! comes to you from Pillsbury's BEST ®Flour. I recommend you use Pillsbury's BEST ®Flour to make all the wonderful recipes in my book!

A note to beginning bakers

Baking bread is exciting. If you follow the directions carefully, step by step, baking bread will be fairly easy. It takes a lot of time, though, so plan to start early in the day so that you won't be rushed.

As with most things, there are rules. Following are some important safety rules which must be followed. Read them over until you understand them completely, then you'll be ready to enjoy the wonderful world of bread baking!

Rules for safety and good bread baking:

1. Ask your parent for permission to bake *before* you start. You might ask them to join you _ perhaps they would like to learn to bake bread also.

2. Wash your hands before you begin. Your hands are important tools which must be kept clean at all times.

3. Be extra careful when you use knives. Put the knife in a safe place away from your work area as soon as you are finished using it.

4. Ask an adult to help you take bread out of a hot oven. Be sure to wear oven gloves.

5. Read all the ingredients for the recipe *before* you begin so that you'll be sure you have everything you need.

6. Protect your clothing. Put on an apron.

7. <u>Be neat</u>. The fun of baking is not so much fun when you have a big mess to clean up afterwards. Clean your area even as you work.

8. *Smile*. This is going to be lots of fun!

BREAD-BAKING TOOLS (Utensils)

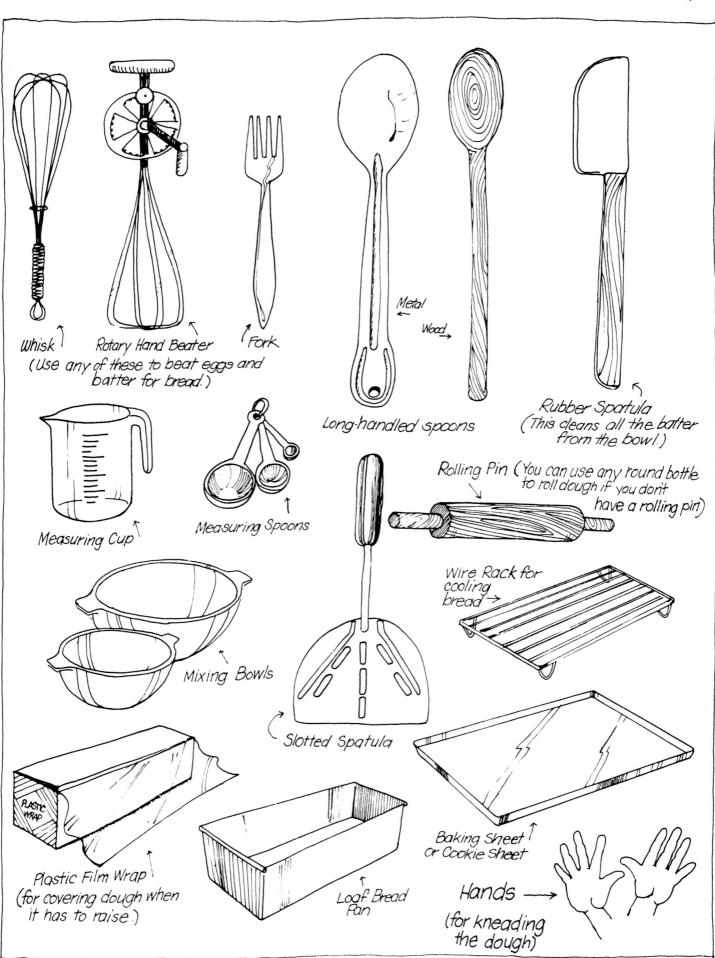

Whisk   Rotary Hand Beater   Fork
(Use any of these to beat eggs and batter for bread.)

Metal ←   Wood →
Long-handled spoons

Rubber Spatula
(This cleans all the batter from the bowl.)

Measuring Cup

Measuring Spoons

Rolling Pin (You can use any round bottle to roll dough if you don't have a rolling pin)

Mixing Bowls

Wire Rack for cooling bread →

Slotted Spatula

PLASTIC WRAP

Plastic Film Wrap
(for covering dough when it has to raise.)

Loaf Bread Pan

Baking Sheet or Cookie Sheet

Hands →
(for kneading the dough)

How Yeast makes the bread dough rise.

Yeast is a living substance of tiny one-celled plants called *fungi*. They are so small we cannot see them without using a microscope. They are everywhere in nature, even in the air we breathe.

<u>How Yeast Works</u>: When yeasts are mixed with water, flour and a little sugar, it begins a chemical change in the sugar which causes tiny gas bubbles to form. This process is called *fermentation*. As the yeast ferments, the little bubbles begin to grow. As they grow, they push the dough up, making the dough grow bigger. When the dough is kept warm, the bubbles keep growing, and the dough gets bigger and bigger.

There's a word for yeast (or baking powder, which we use in some breads instead of yeast). It's called *leavening*. It means *to raise*. So when a recipe says it uses yeast as a *leavener*, it means it uses yeast to make the bread rise.

"Kneading" the dough.
What it means and how to do it.

Many yeast bread recipes ask us to "knead" the dough. When we knead the dough we are pushing the yeast – which makes the bread rise, evenly throughout the dough. Kneading also makes the dough soft and stretchy. It is important to knead the dough well for a good loaf of bread.

As you knead, use your shoulders and the top part of your body and lean into the dough. Don't be too gentle with it. Push down and forward, turn it and push down and forward again! Not only is this fun to do, but good exercise as well.

Step 1. Sprinkle your work area with flour.

Step 2. Place dough onto floured area and sprinkle it with more flour, keeping plenty of flour on your hands.

Step 3. Starting from the part of the dough closest to you, push down and away from you with the heels of your hands.

Step 4. Give the dough one quarter turn, pick up the far end of the dough and pull it up and over towards you. Push down and away again. Repeat this until the dough doesn't feel sticky and is soft and smooth. You may have to add more flour a little at a time if dough gets too sticky to handle.

How mom looks if we leave a mess in the kitchen.

Let's clean up after ourselves. We've got lots of bread to bake! It's more fun for everyone if we are tidy bakers. The first recipe starts on the next page.

ITALIAN BREAD

    This would be a good recipe to start with.
You'll really learn a lot about bread baking, and you'll
enjoy shaping this big crusty loaf.
    Follow each step of the directions carefully
and when this loaf comes out of the oven you'll be
able to call yourself a real bread baker! Good luck!!

WHAT YOU'LL NEED TO MAKE ONE LARGE LOAF:

Utensils
Large bowl
Measuring cup and spoon
Long handled spoon
Small pot
Rolling pin
Baking or cookie sheet
Wire rack

Ingredients
1 envelope active dry yeast
1 teaspoon sugar (or 1 Tablespoon honey)
½ cup warm water
½ stick butter or margarine
½ cup hot water
1 teaspoon salt
3 to 3½ cups unbleached flour
Cornmeal
Vegetable shortening

HOW TO DO IT:

Step 1. Put ½ cup warm water into bowl. Don't make it too hot – test it with your finger – it should be comfortable. Sprinkle on 1 envelope active dry yeast and 1 teaspoon sugar (or 1 Tablespoon honey) and stir until well mixed and the yeast is dissolved.

Step 2. Cut ½ stick butter or margarine into thin slices. Put ½ cup very hot water into small pot. You can take the water from the kitchen faucet if it's very hot, otherwise heat it on the stove. Put butter slices into water to melt.

Step 3. When the butter-water has cooled to lukewarm, add 1 teaspoon salt and stir. Pour this over the dissolved yeast in the large bowl. Stir well.

ITALIAN BREAD

Step 4. Add 1 cup flour and stir with long-handled spoon until well mixed.

Step 5. Add 1 cup flour. Stir well. Add another cup flour and stir until the dough starts to come away from the sides of the bowl.

Step 6. Sprinkle flour on your work area. Scrape dough onto it.

Sprinkle flour onto the dough and onto your hands.

Now press down on dough with both hands, then turn the dough, and press again. Keep doing this until dough becomes easy to handle.

Step 7. Knead the dough (see page 12) for at least 3 minutes. Keep adding flour a little at a time, when the dough gets too sticky. When dough is soft and smooth, let it rest for 5 minutes.

Step 8. Roll the dough into a rectangle shape about 14 inches long and 8 inches wide.

Step 9.  Starting at the wide end, roll the dough up tightly one turn.

Press down firmly along the inside edge of roll with your thumbs. This is called "pinching the seams." It joins the dough together. Continue rolling and pinching the seams until the loaf looks like this

Step 10. Grease a baking sheet with shortening, then sprinkle it with cornmeal. → Place the loaf in the center of the baking sheet with the seam facing down.

Place baking sheet in a warm draft-free place to rise until it gets twice as big. This will take about one hour. 15 minutes before dough has finished rising, put oven on, to 425°.

Step 11. Bake in 425° oven for 35 to 40 minutes. You can tell if it's done if it sounds hollow when you tap it with your knuckles. Use oven gloves to remove from oven. Cool on a wire rack.

· Whole Wheat Loaf ·

You won't have to knead this flavorful loaf of bread. It's made with a batter technique which means you'll have to do a lot of stirring to mix in the yeast.

WHAT YOU'LL NEED:

Utensils
Large bowl
Long-handled spoon
Measuring cup, spoons
Plastic wrap
Loaf pan (9" by 5" by 3")
Wire rack

Ingredients
1 envelope active dry yeast
1½ cups warm water
3 Tablespoons dark molasses or
   3 Tablespoons dark brown sugar
3 Tablespoons salad oil
2 teaspoons salt
1 cup whole wheat flour
1 cup quick-cooking oats (oatmeal)
1½ cups white flour

HOW TO DO IT:

Step 1. Put 1½ cups warm water into a large mixing bowl. Sprinkle on 1 envelope active dry yeast, stir until the yeast is dissolved.

Step 2. Add 3 Tablespoons dark molasses (you can use brown sugar instead), 3 Tablespoons salad oil and 2 teaspoons of salt. Stir until well mixed.

Step 3. Using a long-handled spoon, stir in 1 cup whole wheat flour, a little at a time. Beat this very well for 3 minutes, or at least 200 strokes. This will be a loose batter and will not be hard work -- *yet!*

Step 4. Add 1 cup white flour, stir until all the flour becomes moistened, then beat 100 strokes.

Step 5. Add ½ cup more white flour and 1 cup quick oats (oatmeal) and stir until you have a stiffer batter. Be sure to scrape all the flour from the sides of the bowl into the batter. Beat this at least 175 strokes. This will be hard work. If you get tired, rest a little or, have someone else take a turn. I'll bet you can always find some volunteers!

Wheat Loaf

Step 6. Cover the bowl of batter with plastic wrap and place in a warm place to rise until the batter gets twice as large. This should take about one hour. If it takes longer, don't worry, it just needs more time.

Step 7. Remove the plastic wrap and stir batter 15 strokes.

Step 8. Grease the bread loaf pan with vegetable shortening.

Step 9. Spoon the batter into the pan and spread it as flat as you can.

Now rub some flour on your hands and pat the top of the loaf gently to make it smooth. Careful, the batter will be sticky.

Step 10. Let the dough rise again for 45 minutes. The dough should rise to the rim of the pan.

Step 11. Put the oven on set to 375°. Wait 10 minutes, then put your bread into the oven to bake for 45 to 50 minutes. You'll know it's done when the loaf is nice and brown and sounds hollow when you tap it with your knuckles.

Step 12. Be sure to wear oven gloves when you take your bread from the oven. Keep them on and turn the loaf out of the pan onto a wire rack to cool. (Turn the loaf upright).

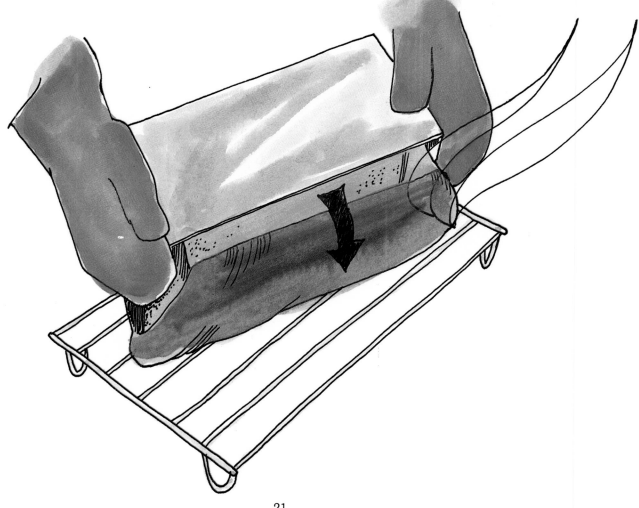

Fancy Shmancy Dinner Rolls

What a *fancy* baker you'll be when you make these beautiful tender dinner rolls.

WHAT YOU'LL NEED TO MAKE 9 LARGE ROLLS:

<u>Utensils</u>

Large mixing bowl
Measuring cup and spoons
Long-handled spoon
Whisk or hand beater
Plastic wrap
Muffin tin

<u>Ingredients</u>

1 envelope active dry yeast
2½ to 3 cups white flour
1 teaspoon salt
2 Tablespoons sugar
¾ cup hot water
2 Tablespoons salad oil
1 egg

HOW TO DO IT:

Step 1. Put 1 cup flour, 1 envelope dry yeast, 1 teaspoon salt and 2 Tablespoons sugar into a large bowl. Stir until well mixed.

Step 2. Pour ¾ cup hot water (which you can take directly from the faucet) over the flour mixture. Add 2 Tablespoons salad oil and one egg.
Mix with a long-handled spoon until all the flour becomes moist. Beat with a hand egg beater or whisk until it becomes a smooth batter. About 120 strokes.

Step 3. Cover the bowl with plastic wrap and let it rest in a warm place (like an unlit oven) for 15 minutes.

Step 4. Add 1½ cups of flour, a little at a time, stirring with a long-handled spoon until you have a soft, sticky dough. Sprinkle your work area with flour and scrape the dough onto it.

Fancy Shmancy

Step 5. Sprinkle the dough with flour, and, leaving flour on your hands, knead the dough. Add more flour a little at a time, when the dough gets too sticky. Knead 3 or 4 minutes until dough is nice and smooth.

Step 6. Cut dough into three equal pieces.

Step 7. Cut each piece into three again. Now you have nine.

Step 8. Grease nine cups of a muffin tin with vegetable shortening.

Step 9. Cut each piece of dough into three <u>again</u>! Roll each little piece in your hands to form a little ball.

Put 3 dough balls into each greased muffin cup and press them gently into place.

Step 10. Put the rolls in a warm place to rise until they get twice as big. This should take about 30 minutes.

Step 11. Put the oven on, set to 425°. Wait 10 minutes, then put the rolls in to bake until they are golden brown. This will take 10 to 15 minutes. Don't forget to use oven gloves when you take the rolls from the hot oven. Serve them warm with butter.

This is only the start of your bread baking experience. Once you have learned the basics in this book you can become very creative with your breads. You can choose from a variety of flours*for different tastes and textures. However this wasn't always the way it was.

In 1847 a baker and lecturer named Sylvester Graham introduced a new kind of bread. It was made from finely ground flour which contained the entire wheat kernel including the skin. The other bakers used only sifted white flour for their bread and weren't used to this "whole wheat" taste. They got so upset with him that they started riots, threatened his life and tried to drive him out of business (and probably out of town)!

Fortunately Mr. Graham persisted and today graham flour as it came to be known, makes delicious breads and rolls as well as the popular graham cracker.

* Bread flours are made from a variety of grains in addition to wheat. They include barley, rice, corn, rye, oats and soybeans.

JUMBO BREAD STICKS

You can be very creative with bread sticks. You can make long ones or short ones, fat ones or thin ones. You might even want to try S-shapes or bows. Use your imagination, but perhaps it would be best to make straight ones the first time.

WHAT YOU'LL NEED TO MAKE 12 JUMBO BREAD STICKS:

Utensils

Large mixing bowl
Measuring cup and spoons
Long-handled spoon
2 baking sheets

Ingredients

2 cups unbleached white flour
1 envelope active dry yeast
2 teaspoons sugar
2 Tablespoons olive or salad oil

½ teaspoon salt
¾ cup hot water
oil-to grease 2 baking sheets

HOW TO DO IT:

Step 1. Put 1 cup flour, 2 teaspoons sugar, ½ teaspoon salt and 1 envelope active dry yeast into a large mixing bowl. Stir until well mixed.

Step 2. Put ¾ cup hot water - right from the kitchen faucet - into a measuring cup. Add 2 Tablespoons of salad oil and pour this over the flour mixture in the large bowl. Stir with a long-handled spoon, scraping all the flour into the batter from the sides of the bowl. Beat until smooth, about 60 strokes.

Step 3. Add ½ cup flour and blend until smooth.

Step 4. Add another ½ cup flour and stir until batter forms a soft dough.

Step 5. Sprinkle your work area with flour and scrape the dough onto it. Put plenty of flour on your hands and knead the dough until it feels nice and smooth. This should take 3 or 4 minutes. Add more flour if the dough gets too sticky.

Step 6. Shape the dough into a roll about 8 inches long. Then cut it in half.

BREAD STICKS

Step 7. Cut each of the halves in half again. Now you have four pieces.

Cut each of these pieces into three, so that now you have 12 pieces.

Step 8. Roll each piece of dough into a rope shape about 14 inches long. If the dough doesn't stretch easily, let it rest for a few minutes, then continue.

Step 9. Grease 2 baking sheets with oil. Use olive oil if you have it, otherwise salad oil.

Step 10. Place the ropes of dough onto the oiled baking sheets, rolling them as you do this. This allows the breadstick to become oiled on all sides.

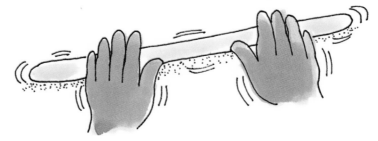

Space them one inch apart, six on a sheet.

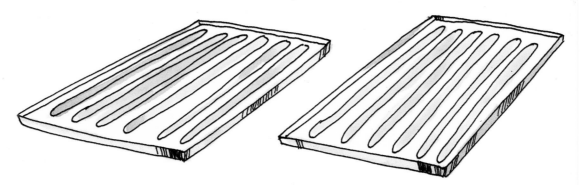

Step 11. Cover the breadsticks with plastic wrap. Place them in a warm place to rise, for 30 minutes.

Step 12. After 20 minutes, (about 10 minutes before the breadsticks are finished rising), put the oven on to heat to 375°. (Be sure to take the breadsticks out, if that's where you put them to rise.)

Step 13. Remove the plastic wrap and bake the breadsticks in 375° oven for 15 to 20 minutes. They are done when they are light brown all over.

YUM!

NO·KNEAD DINNER ROLLS

This recipe makes a light, tender dinner roll that you don't have to knead.

WHAT YOU NEED TO MAKE 12 ROLLS:

Utensils	Ingredients
Sauce pan	2¼ cups white unbleached flour
Large mixing bowl	2 Tablespoons sugar
Measuring cups and spoons	1 envelope active dry yeast
Hand egg beater or whisk	1 teaspoon salt
Long-handled spoon	1 cup milk
Plastic wrap	1 egg
Muffin tins	½ stick butter or margarine
	Shortening to grease tins

HOW TO DO IT:

Step 1. Put one cup milk into a saucepan. Cut ½ stick of butter or margarine into slices, then drop them into the milk. Heat milk on <u>low</u> until butter is half melted. <u>Do not boil</u>. Take pan off stove.

Step 2. In a large bowl, put 1 envelope yeast, 1 cup flour, 2 Tablespoons sugar and 1 teaspoon salt. Stir to mix.

Step 3. Pour milk and butter mixture which should be warm, but not hot, into bowl of flour mixture. Add 1 egg and beat with a whisk or egg-beater for 3 minutes. This will not be a heavy batter so this will be easy to beat well.

Step 4. Add 1¼ cups flour a little at a time, as you stir with a long-handled spoon. Scrape the sides of the bowl to get all of the dry flour into the wet batter.
   Keep stirring until it becomes a smooth batter. This will be hard work, because the batter will be stiff, but it is important to stir it well.

Step 5. Cover bowl with plastic wrap and put in a warm place to rise until it gets twice as big. This will take from 45 minutes to 1 hour.

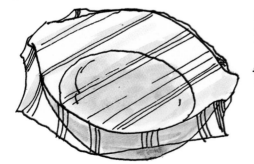

Step 6. Grease 12 cups of muffin tins with vegetable shortening.

Step 7. When the batter has finished rising, stir it 10 times with a long-handled spoon, to break gas bubbles.

NO·KNEAD ROLLS

Step 8. Spoon batter into greased muffin cups, filling them about half-full.

Let the dough rise again for about 45 minutes.

Step 9. After rolls have risen, put oven on to 400°. Wait 10 minutes, then put rolls in to bake until golden brown. This will take from 10 to 15 minutes.

Step 10. Remove from oven (don't forget to wear oven gloves). Let cool on a wire rack for a few minutes.

Prehistoric people made hard, flat, unraised bread by mixing grain meals and water to form a dough which they baked on hot rocks that they heated.

Then over 4000 years ago, about 2600 BC, the ancient Egyptians learned how to make raised bread by mixing grain flour with water and let it sit in a warm place for a long time. This caused the mixture to ferment, and they used this fermented mixture to make the bread rise. They didn't understand how this process worked, but they liked this lighter more flavorful bread better. It was the tiny microscopic yeast plants (fungi) that are in the air... in the grain... everywhere in nature...that caused it to happen.

WHEN WILL IT BE READY? I'M STARVING!

In fact it wasn't until about 4000 years later that Dr. Louis Pasteur in his experiments with fermentation, discovered what yeast is. And today yeast is packaged for us in blocks like butter or little foil envelopes – just waiting for us to mix it with flour and water to help us make all kinds of delicious breads.

AH-HA! EETS YEAST!

PIZZA TALK

IN THE NEIGHBORHOOD WHERE I GREW UP— THERE WERE MANY WONDERFUL ITALIAN PIZZA BAKERS.

THEY COULD DO SO MANY TRICKS WITH THE PIZZA DOUGH IN ORDER TO STRETCH IT.

THEY'D TOSS IT UP AND SPIN IT IN THE AIR...

AND THEY'D STRETCH IT LIKE THIS... BUT THE MOST IMPORTANT THING WAS— WHILE THEY MADE THE PIZZA, THEY ALWAYS SAID THE WORD "PIZZA" WITH AN ITALIAN ACCENT, WHICH SOUNDED TO ME LIKE "AH-BEETS!"

SO LET'S MAKE A PIZZA TOGETHER— BUT BEFORE WE DO, LET'S ALL SHOUT AH-BEETS! READY?...

AH BEETS!

WHAT YOU'LL NEED TO MAKE ONE PIZZA:

Utensils

Large mixing bowl
Small mixing bowl
Measuring cup and spoons
Long handled spoon
Whisk or hand beater
Baking sheet (at least 10½" by
    15½") or large round
    pizza pan

Ingredients for dough

1 envelope active dry yeast
1 teaspoon sugar
1 teaspoon salt
1 cup warm water
2 Tablespoons salad oil
2½ cups unbleached flour

Ingredients for pizza topping

1½ cups crushed tomatoes or
    tomato sauce.
2 Tablespoons salad oil
2 heaping Tablespoons grated
    parmesan or romano cheese
½ teaspoon oregano
¼ teaspoon garlic powder
8 oz. (½ lb.) mozzarella cheese
½ teaspoon salt

HOW TO DO IT:

Step 1. Put one cup warm - not hot - water, 1 teaspoon sugar
into large mixing bowl. Sprinkle on 1 envelope
active dry yeast. Stir well until yeast is dissolved.

Step 2. Add 1 teaspoon salt and
2 Tablespoons salad oil and
stir well. Add 1 cup flour
and stir until all the flour
is moist, then beat with
a whisk or hand beater until you get
a smooth batter. About 150 strokes.

Step 3. Add 1½ cups flour, a little at a time, stirring with your long-handled spoon until the flour gets mixed into the batter and forms a ball of dough which will pull away from the sides of the bowl.

Step 4. Sprinkle your work area with flour and scrape dough onto it. Sprinkle top of dough with more flour and knead dough for about 4 minutes or until the dough becomes very soft and smooth. Add more flour a little at a time if dough becomes too sticky and hard to handle.

Step 5. Wash and dry the large mixing bowl. Put 1 Tablespoon salad oil into it. Place the dough in the bowl and turn it over so that it becomes covered with oil on all sides. Cover the bowl with plastic wrap and place in a warm place, like an unlit oven, to rise until it gets twice as big... about one hour.

Step 6. Punch down the dough in the bowl. This releases the gas bubbles. Cover dough again with the plastic wrap. Let rise again for 45 minutes. While dough is rising, prepare your pizza sauce.

Step 7. PIZZA SAUCE

Put 1½ cups crushed tomatoes or tomato sauce into a small mixing bowl. Add 2 Tablespoons salad oil, 2 heaping Tablespoons grated cheese, ½ teaspoon oregano, ½ teaspoon salt, and ¼ teaspoon garlic powder. Stir to mix.

Step 8. Put oven on to 450°. (Be sure to take out the rising dough if that's where you put it.)

Step 9. Cut ½ lb. (8 oz.) mozzarella cheese into strips, or any small shaped pieces. You can do this easily by first cutting the cheese into slices, then pile up the slices and cut them into strips.

Step 10. Grease the pizza pan with vegetable shortening.

Step 11. Sprinkle flour lightly on your work area. Place the fully risen dough onto it. Press the dough flat with your hands. (Press it into a circle if you're using a round pan, or a rectangle for a baking sheet.)

Step 12. Pick the dough up and stretch it slightly, pulling from the center. Be careful that you don't pull so much that you tear the dough. Place the dough in the center of the pan and press from the middle towards the edge of the pan.

Leave the edge thicker to form the crust. If you tear the dough, don't worry – just "pinch" the edges of the tear together.

Step 13. Spoon the sauce evenly onto the dough. Be careful not to go too close to the edge - leave about ½ inch for the crust. Now sprinkle the mozzarella cheese evenly over the sauce. Looks like pizza now, right?

Step 14. Bake in 450° oven for 15 or 20 minutes or until crust is golden brown and the cheese is bubbly. Remove from oven - be sure to wear oven gloves – let rest for 5 minutes. Cut into slices and shout "AH-BEETS!"

PEPPY PEPPERONI BREAD

This dinner bread not only tastes different, it looks different. It's delicious served warm. If you're lucky enough to have any left over for the next day, the rest should be kept in the refrigerator... wrapped in a towel or put in a plastic bag.

WHAT YOU'LL NEED TO MAKE ONE LOAF:

Utensils: Large mixing bowl
Measuring cup, spoons
Long-handled spoon
Whisk or hand beater
Baking sheet
Plastic wrap
Wire rack

Ingredients: 1 envelope dry yeast
½ cup warm water
1 teaspoon sugar
1 teaspoon salt
1-8-oz. can tomato sauce
3 Tablespoons salad oil
3 Tablespoons grated parmesan cheese
3 cups unbleached flour
¼ lb. sliced pepperoni

HOW TO DO IT:

Step 1. Put ½ cup warm, not hot, water into a large mixing bowl. Sprinkle in 1 envelope active dry yeast and 1 teaspoon sugar. Stir until the yeast is dissolved.

Step 2. Add 3 Tablespoons salad oil, 1 small 8 oz. can tomato sauce (or 1 cup). Stir until well mixed.

Step 3. Add 3 heaping Tablespoons of grated parmesan cheese, and 1½ cups flour. Stir until the flour becomes moist, then beat with a whisk or hand beater until you get a smooth batter. (150 strokes)

Step 4. Add another 1½ cups of flour, a little at a time, stirring with a long-handled spoon until the flour is mixed into the batter and forms a ball of dough. The dough will pull away from the sides of the bowl.

Step 5. Sprinkle your work area with flour and scrape the dough onto it. Sprinkle more flour onto the dough and knead until the dough gets soft and smooth. This will take about 4 minutes. Add a little more flour if the dough gets too sticky and hard to handle.

Step 6. Cover the dough with plastic wrap and let it rest 10 minutes on your work surface. Go on to Step 7.

Step 7. Peel and slice 4 ounces of pepperoni into thin slices. (Many deli's and supermarkets sell it already sliced.) Then cut each slice in half and each half in half again. You can stack 3 or 4 slices and cut them at the same time.

Step 8. Press down in the center of the dough to make a little bowl shape. Put the pepperoni pieces into the bowl, then fold the dough up over the pepperoni. Knead the dough to mix the pepperoni throughout. Some pieces will fall out – just push them back in.

Step 9. Grease a baking sheet with vegetable shortening. Shape the dough into a loaf and place it on the baking sheet. Let it rise until it gets twice as big. This will take about one hour. After about 45 minutes, put the oven on to 425°.

Step 10. Bake in 425° oven 30-35 minutes, or until the bread sounds hollow when you tap it with your knuckles. Let cool on wire rack for 5 minutes before slicing.

Bagels are really fun to make, but you should ask an adult to help you because the bagels have to be boiled in water before they are baked. Start early in the day. There are a lot of steps to this recipe... but it's worth it — they're great!

WHAT YOU'LL NEED TO MAKE NINE BAGELS:

<u>Utensils</u>

2 mixing bowls
Measuring spoons and cup
Plastic wrap
Long-handled spoon
2 baking sheets
Slotted spoon
Large pot (5 or 6 quart)
Pastry brush or napkin
Towel
Wire rack

<u>Ingredients</u>

1 envelope active dry yeast
1 cup warm water
2 Tablespoons sugar
1 heaping teaspoon salt
3 cups white flour
3 quarts water with 1 Tablespoon sugar
Cornmeal
1 egg yolk with 1 Tablespoon water
Vegetable shortening

HOW TO DO IT:

Step 1. Put 1 cup warm, not hot, water in large mixing bowl. Sprinkle 1 envelope yeast, 2 Tablespoons sugar and 1 heaping teaspoon salt into the water. Stir until dissolved.

Step 2. Add 2 cups of flour a little at a time, and beat well with a long-handled spoon until you have a smooth batter.

Step 3. Add ½ cup more flour. Stir until dough gets stiffer.

Step 4. Sprinkle flour on your work area. Scrape dough onto it.

Sprinkle flour onto dough and onto your hands. Knead the dough until it is smooth. This will be hard work because the dough will be firmer than most bread doughs. Keep adding flour a little at a time when dough gets too sticky. Knead for 10 minutes.

Step 5. Grease a bowl with vegetable shortening and place dough into it. Turn the dough over so that it gets covered with shortening on all sides. Cover the bowl with plastic wrap and place in a warm place, (like an unlit gas oven) to rise until it gets twice as big. This usually takes about one hour

Step 6. Punch dough down to release gas bubbles.

Then slide the dough onto a lightly floured work area. Knead for one minute.

BAGELS!

Step 7. Shape dough into a square, then cut into 9 equal pieces.

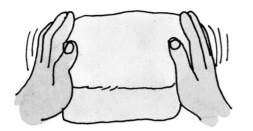 

Step 8. Knead each piece a little, then form into a smooth ball.

Step 9. Hold the dough ball with both hands, and poke your thumbs through the center. With one thumb in the hole, shape like a doughnut.

Step 10. Place bagels on flat plates which have been sprinkled with flour. Put them in a warm place for 20 minutes.

Step 11. Lightly grease <u>two</u> baking sheets with shortening. Sprinkle them with corn meal.

Step 12. Put 3 quarts of water into a large pot. Add 1 Tablespoon sugar. Heat until water boils, then lower heat so that the water boils gently.

Step 13. Put oven on to 400.°

Step 14. Gently lift one bagel at a time, using a flat spatula. Ask an adult to help you place the bagel into the boiling water. Boil two or three at a time for 5 minutes, turning them often.

Step 15. With a slotted spoon, lift the bagels out of the water and place on a cloth towel. This is to drain the extra water.

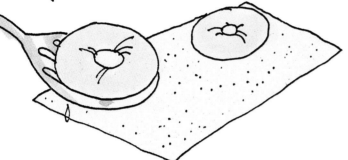

After they have drained, place them on greased baking sheets.

Step 16. With a fork or whisk, beat 1 egg yolk with 1 Tablespoon water. Brush each bagel with this mixture, using a pastry brush or a rolled-up napkin as a brush.

Step 17. Bake bagels at 400° for 25 minutes or until they are golden brown. Use oven gloves to take them from the oven, cool on a wire rack. *Mmmmm!*

COFFEE CAN BREAD

This bread is baked in coffee cans! Even the plastic lids that come on the coffee cans are used. They tell you when the dough has risen enough and is ready to go into the oven for baking...because they pop off!

WHAT YOU'LL NEED TO MAKE TWO LOAVES:

Utensils
Large mixing bowl
Measuring cup and spoons
Long-handled spoon
2 one pound size coffee cans
(with plastic lids)
Wire cooling rack

Ingredients
1 envelope active dry yeast
½ cup warm water
3 Tablespoons sugar
1 large (13 oz) can evaporated milk
1 teaspoon salt
2 Tablespoons salad oil
4 cups unbleached white flour
vegetable shortening

HOW TO DO IT:

Step 1. In a large bowl, put ½ cup warm, but not hot water. Sprinkle in one envelope dry yeast and 1 Tablespoon sugar. Stir until yeast is dissolved. Let stand for 15 minutes or until it gets bubbly.

Step 2. Add 2 Tablespoons sugar, 1 can (13 oz) evaporated milk, 1 teaspoon salt and 2 Tablespoons salad oil. Stir well.

Step 3. With a long-handled spoon, stir in 2 cups flour a little at a time, and beat well, about 150 strokes. The batter should be nice and smooth.

Step 4. Add 1 cup flour and stir well, scraping all of the flour into the batter from the sides of the bowl. Now you have a heavier sticky batter. Beat until smooth. This will be hard work. If you get tired, rest a little or have someone else take a turn.

Step 5. Add 1 more cup flour and mix well into the batter. Now this is really hard work, but keep stirring until all the flour is mixed well into the batter and it is nice and smooth.

Yay! The hard part is over and the fun part begins!

COFFEE CAN BREAD

Step 6. Grease two 1 pound coffee cans and the undersides of 2 plastic lids with vegetable shortening.

Step 7. Spoon half the batter into each of the cans.

Step 8. Cover each can with a greased lid.
Place the covered cans in a warm draft-free place like an unlit oven, until the batter rises, and the lids pop up.

This should take about one hour, but don't worry if it takes longer. Sometimes the yeast gets lazy if it's not as warm as it likes. Just keep the cans where they are until the lids pop.

Step 9. Take the cans out of the oven, if that's where you put them. Remove the oven's top shelf, and put the oven on to 350°. (Handle the cans gently if and when you move them.)

Step 10. Place the cans gently into 350° oven. Bake for 45 minutes. The crust will be very brown.

Step 11. Take the bread out of the oven (be sure to use oven gloves) and place on a wire rack to cool for 10 minutes.

Step 12. Slide bread out of cans by giving them a little twist, then pulling them out.

If they are difficult to remove from can, loosen around the rim with a small, thin knife blade.

Place loaves standing up on wire rack to finish cooling.

Introducing
Quick Breads.

Now *that's* a silly illustration for Quick Breads! Quick Breads do not zip out of the oven at all. However, they do take much less time to prepare, because they do not use yeast as a leavener (to make the dough rise). They usually use baking powder in the dough which means the dough does not have to rise *first*, before baking, like yeast breads... all of the rising is done in the oven as the bread is baking. Just mix all the ingredients, shape or pour the dough into the pan and bake in a pre-heated oven... *and presto!*... wonderful bread is on the way.

The recipes that follow are quick bread recipes.

CORNY CAPERS

CORNY CORN BREAD

This recipe makes delicious corn bread. It makes delicious corn muffins also. Just spoon the bread batter into greased muffin tins - halfway up - and bake in 425° oven for 15 - 20 minutes.

WHAT YOU'LL NEED FOR ONE SQUARE CORN BREAD:

Utensils
2 mixing bowls
Measuring spoons; cup.
Long-handled spoon
Fork or whisk
8 or 9 inch square pan

Ingredients
1¼ cups white unbleached flour
¾ cup corn meal
2 Tablespoons sugar
4 teaspoons baking powder
1 teaspoon salt
2 eggs
1 cup milk
4 Tablespoons salad oil

HOW TO DO IT:

Step 1. Put oven on, set to 425°.

Step 2. Into a large mixing bowl, put 1¼ cups flour, ¾ cup corn meal, 2 Tablespoons sugar, 4 teaspoons baking powder, and 1 teaspoon salt. Stir with a long handled spoon until well mixed. Shape a well in center of dry mixture. ↑

Step 3. Into a small bowl put 1 cup milk, 2 eggs and 4 Tablespoons salad oil. Beat with a whisk or fork.

Step 4. Pour egg mixture into the well you made in the flour mixture. →

Stir well, using a long-handled spoon. This should be a smooth, creamy batter. ↓

Step 5. Grease an 8 or 9 inch square baking pan with vegetable shortening.

Step 6. Scrape batter into pan. Bake in 425° oven for 20-25 minutes. Cut into squares and serve warm with butter.

Irish Soda Bread

What St. Patty's Day would be complete without soda bread? But this bread is too good to have only once a year.

We use baking powder and baking soda to make the bread rise.

Slice it nice and thin and serve with butter. You can make it with or without raisins.

WHAT YOU'LL NEED:

Utensils
2 Mixing bowls
Measuring cup and spoons
Long-handled spoon
Fork or whisk
Sauce pan
1 pie plate (or cookie sheet)

Ingredients
2½ cups unbleached white flour
½ teaspoon salt
1½ teaspoons baking powder
½ teaspoon baking soda
2 Tablespoons sugar
2 Tablespoons butter or margarine
1 egg
1 cup milk
1 teaspoon lemon juice
1 cup raisins
¼ teaspoon caraway seeds
vegetable shortening

HOW TO DO IT:

Step 1. Put oven on set to 375°

Step 2. In a large bowl put 2½ cups unbleached flour, ½ teaspoon salt, 1½ teaspoons baking powder, ½ teaspoon baking soda and 2 Tablespoons sugar. Stir until well mixed. Set aside.

Step 3. Put 2 Tablespoons butter or margarine into a small sauce pan. Heat on low flame until melted. Let cool.

Step 4. In another bowl beat 1 egg with a fork or whisk. Add 1 cup milk and 1 teaspoon lemon juice. Stir to mix.

Step 5. Pour the melted butter into the egg-milk mixture and stir to mix.

Step 6. Pour this mixture into the bowl with the flour, and with a long-handled spoon, stir until all the flour becomes moistened. Add 1 cup raisins and ¼ teaspoon caraway seeds. Mix well.

Step 7. Sprinkle flour onto your work area. Scrape dough onto it. Sprinkle flour on your hands and onto the dough. Knead until smooth, about 3 minutes. <u>Add more flour if dough gets too sticky.</u>

Step 8. Shape the dough into a smooth round ball.

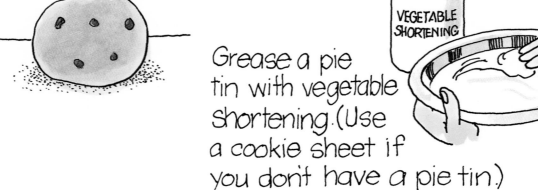

Grease a pie tin with vegetable shortening. (Use a cookie sheet if you don't have a pie tin.)

VEGETABLE SHORTENING

Step 9. Place the dough into the tin and press down to flatten the top until dough almost reaches the sides of pan.

Step 10. With a sharp knife that has been dipped in flour, cut a cross ½ inch deep across the top of loaf. Bake in 375° oven 35-40 minutes – until brown and crusty.

PAPER BAG BREAD

This is a sweet, cake-like bread that's baked in an ordinary plain brown lunch bag. It uses baking powder as a leavening to make it rise.

WHAT YOU'LL NEED FOR ONE PAPER BAG BREAD:

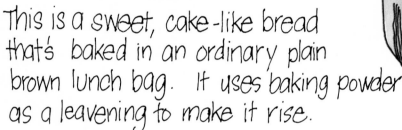

Utensils

2 large mixing bowls
Measuring cups and spoons
Long-handled spoon
Hand beater or fork
Baking sheet
1 paper lunch bag
    (3½ inches by 5½ inches)
Small sauce pan

Ingredients

½ cup (1 stick) butter or margarine
2 eggs
¾ cup sugar
1 teaspoon cinnamon
½ teaspoon ground nutmeg
¼ cup raisins
¼ cup chopped walnuts
2¾ cups white unbleached flour
2 teaspoons baking powder
½ teaspoon salt
1 cup milk
Vegetable shortening

PAPER BAG

HOW TO DO IT:

Step 1. In a small sauce pan melt 1 stick butter or margarine. Let cool.

Step 2. In a large bowl, beat 2 eggs and ¾ cup sugar together, using a whisk or fork. Pour in the melted butter, add 1 teaspoon cinnamon, ½ teaspoon nutmeg and beat this mixture together. Add ¼ cup raisins and ¼ cup chopped walnuts. Blend well, using a long-handled spoon.

Step 3. In another large bowl, put 2¾ cups flour, 2 teaspoons baking powder, ½ teaspoon salt. Stir until well mixed.

Step 4. Add half the flour mixture to the egg mixture and stir with a long-handled spoon, about 50 strokes.

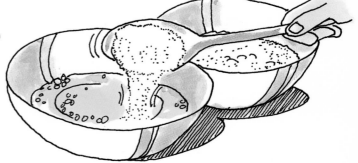

Step 5. Add ½ cup milk and stir until well blended.

Step 6. Add the rest of the flour mixture and another ½ cup milk. Stir until blended, then beat 50 strokes.

Step 7. Take top rack out of oven. Set oven to 325°.

Step 8. Fold the top of a paper bag down, to form a cuff about 3 inches deep.

Step 9. Now comes the yukky part! Grease the inside of the paper bag with vegetable shortening. Be sure you don't miss any spots.

Put oven on to 325°

Step 10. Set bag on a cookie or baking sheet and pour in the batter.

Step 11. Bake in 325° oven for 1 hour and 35 minutes. The bread should be well browned.

Step 12. Let bread cool for 10 minutes, then tear off the paper, cut into wedges and enjoy while it's still warm.

UGLY BISCUITS

Ohhh, are these biscuits U-G-L-Y!.. but they sure taste good.
   They're quick and easy to make. You can begin about one half hour before dinner and serve them piping hot from the oven.

WHAT YOU'LL NEED TO MAKE TWELVE UGLY BISCUITS:

Utensils
Sauce pan
Mixing bowl
Fork
Long-handled spoon
Measuring cup and spoons
Cookie sheet
Tablespoon

Ingredients
1½ cups white flour
1 Tablespoon baking powder
½ stick butter or margarine
½ cup milk
½ teaspoon salt
Vegetable shortening

HOW TO DO IT:

Step 1. Put oven on to 450°.

Step 2. Melt ½ stick butter or margarine in small saucepan.

Step 3. Put 1½ cups flour, ½ teaspoon salt, 1 Tablespoon baking powder into a mixing bowl. Stir until well mixed.

Step 4. Slowly pour melted butter over flour mixture, stirring with a fork as you do this. Stir until everything looks crumbly and there are no large lumps. Break up any large pieces with the side of the fork.

Step 5. Pour ½ cup milk in, and stir with the fork just until everything becomes moistened. You'll have a very lumpy heavy batter.

Step 6. Grease a cookie sheet lightly with vegetable shortening.

Step 7. Scoop up a heaping Tablespoon of batter and drop onto baking sheet, space them just a little bit apart. You should have enough batter to make twelve biscuits.

Step 8. Bake for 10 minutes in 450° oven. They will not get too brown. In fact, they look kind of pale, even though they're done. What can you expect from <u>ugly</u> biscuits!... but wait until you taste them...warm, with butter. Mmmmm.

Mash·a·Banana Bread (Whole wheat·banana·nut)

This is a moist dessert bread. It gets its delicious flavor from nuts, whole wheat and fresh ripe bananas.

WHAT YOU'LL NEED FOR ONE LOAF:

Utensils
Sauce pan
2 large mixing bowls
Fork
Measuring cup and spoons
Long-handled spoon
Loaf pan (9" by 5")
Wire rack

Ingredients
1 stick butter or margarine
1 cup sugar
2 eggs
3 ripe bananas
1 cup white flour
½ teaspoon salt
1 cup whole wheat flour
1 teaspoon baking soda
⅓ cup hot water
½ cup chopped walnuts
Vegetable shortening

HOW TO DO IT:

Step 1. Put oven on to 325°. Melt 1 stick butter or margarine (in small sauce pan over low heat). Add 1 cup sugar. Stir to mix well.

Step 2. In a large bowl, beat 2 eggs together with a fork. Pour the butter-sugar mixture in and stir well.

Step 3. In another bowl, mash 3 very ripe bananas with a fork until they become mushy. Stir with a long-handled spoon to make a paste. Pour in the butter-egg mixture and stir until well blended.

Step 4. Add 1 cup white flour, ½ teaspoon salt, 1 teaspoon baking soda and stir until well mixed.

Step 5. Add 1 cup whole wheat flour and ⅓ cup hot water taken from kitchen faucet. Stir until well mixed.

Step 6. Stir in ½ cup chopped walnuts. Keep stirring until you have a smooth batter.

Step 7. Grease a 9 inch by 5 inch loaf pan with vegetable shortening.

Step 8. Spoon the batter into the pan and bake in 325° oven for about 1 hour and 10 minutes. You will see the bread pull away from the sides of the pan. Let the bread cool in the pan for 10 minutes, then take it out of pan and put on a wire rack to finish cooling.

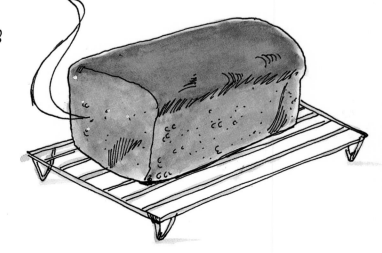

I hope you've enjoyed this bread book as much as I've enjoyed bringing it to you. Bet you're a real bread baker now. The exciting part is — it's just the beginning. There are so many wonderful breads to discover. Ryes, pumpernickels, oatmeal, graham-a**nd** all the ones you can create your**self**!

I'd love to hear from you. Let me know how you're doing with your bread baking. Please write to me at:

HAPPIBOOK PRESS
P.O. Box 218,
Montgomery, New York 12549-0218

Until we meet again, 'bye, it's been fun!

Uncle Gene